CW00501966

MANAGING MONEY GOD'S WAY

A 31-Day Devotional

BOB LOTICH

Copyright © 2015 Rendren Publishing

All rights reserved.

ISBN: 0989894525

ISBN-13: 978-0-9898945-2-4

TABLE OF
CONTENTS

NOTE FROM THE AUTHOR:

This devotional's goal is just to get you pondering the things of God as they pertain to your finances.

Parts of this book are excerpts taken from my writing on SeedTime.com over the last few years, and if you're familiar with my writing style already, you know that I often write in a very personal tone as if I'm speaking to a close friend.

I don't claim to know all the answers, and I'm far from perfect. What I am is a follower of Christ endeavoring to be pleasing to God with my finances and all other areas of my life.

I hope you find the devotional helpful, and if you do I would love to hear from you. And even if you don't, I would love to hear from you, too!

God bless,

Bob

Day 1

Learning how to be content

I have always had a feeling that contentment was a critical component of having joy in life. But lately I have seen a new angle on a few verses in Philippians 4.

Not that I speak from want, for I have learned to be content in whatever circumstances I am. I know how to get along with humble means, and I also know how to live in prosperity; in any and every circumstance I have learned the secret of being filled and going hungry, both of having abundance and suffering need.

Philippians 4:11-12 (NASB)

What exactly was Paul talking about when he said

he knew how to get along with humble means and prosperity?

I'm sure that for him it was a bit of a challenging process to be content living in humble means. He was basically on the fast-track to become a super-Pharisee; from what I understand they were a very materialistic bunch. Then Jesus steps in, and his life is forever changed. And a few years later we see him in prison writing that we should "rejoice in the Lord always" and be content in every circumstance.

Breaking the attachment to things

The first way I look at the "knowhow" that Paul referred to is more of an internal lesson that we need to learn. It's that things are just things. They come, they go. They don't determine your value or worth, and you can't take them with you when you die.

Paul had some of the most tremendous ups and downs. One minute he was shackled hand and foot in prison, and the next he was staying in the King's palace. He seemed to live the full spectrum of having a lot and having a little.

But, his outlook proves that he broke his

attachment to things. He didn't consider his life a failure and quit when he frequently found himself in prison. And on the other hand, he didn't allow more prosperous times to be the pinnacle achievement he would hang his hat on. His goal was to fulfill what God had called him to, and things were just peripheral, so as they came and went he learned not to care too much. He was successfully living Matthew 6:33.

Practically living with a little or a lot

In addition to the internal lesson, I'm starting to suspect there's a practical element to what he's saying as well. Could it be that Paul is also referring to the resourcefulness required when times are tight? On a practical level, managing money is a lot different when you have a lot of it from when you have a little.

If Warren Buffett spent two hours of his work-day cutting grocery coupons to save $10 at the grocery store, it would be a pretty foolish use of his time. He could probably use those same two hours to do what he does so well and make many thousands of dollars. On the other hand, if you're only making $100 a week, it might be worth spending those two hours cutting coupons to save $10.

My wife and I both had the painful experience of living well (and spending more money than we had) and then having to be honest with ourselves and lower our standard of living to what it really is. It isn't fun at all, but trying to live as if you're "in prosperity" when you're in a season of "humble means" is a path toward destruction.

What I have been getting out of Philippians 4:12 is that if I continue to try to live as if I'm rich, when I'm not, then I'm only deceiving myself. For me, moving from having abundance back down to humble means was a test from God. I think he wanted to see whether I would still love Him if I didn't have a lot of stuff. So I had to make many cuts to my lifestyle. I had to go without things I had previously taken for granted. And I had to start praying and trusting God for things that were previously commonplace.

As I said, it was a painful process. But all along I knew it was just a season and that God had more for me. As a result of those lessons we went from debt-ridden over-spenders to a couple who consistently spends less than they earn, has no consumer debt, and who saved a 20% down payment for their house.

One last thing

Just to clarify, I don't believe that contentment means settling for mediocrity. Rather it's being satisfied at whatever place in life God has us, while trusting that He does have our interests at heart and that He does want to bless us and see us succeed. So, I'm trying to learn these lessons that Paul did and be content in my present circumstances, while trusting that God is taking me from glory to glory.

DAY 2

The Parable of the Talents

Jesus' famous parable has a lot to teach us about our money if we let it. Below is the parable and a few of my thoughts about it.

For it is just like a man about to go on a journey, who called his own slaves and entrusted his possessions to them. "To one he gave five talents, to another, two, and to another, one, each according to his own ability; and he went on his journey.
Immediately the one who had received the five talents went and traded with them, and gained five more talents. In the same manner the one who had received the two talents gained two more. But he who received the one talent went away, and dug a

hole in the ground and hid his master's money.
Now after a long time the master of those slaves
came and settled accounts with them. The one who
had received the five talents came up and brought
five more talents, saying, "Master, you entrusted
five talents to me. See, I have gained five more
talents." His master said to him, "Well done, good
and faithful slave You were faithful with a few
things, I will put you in charge of many things;
enter into the joy of your master."
Also the one who had received the two talents
came up and said, "Master, you entrusted two
talents to me. See, I have gained two more talents."
His master said to him, "Well done, good and
faithful slave. You were faithful with a few things, I
will put you in charge of many things; enter into
the joy of your master."
And the one also who had received the one talent
came up and said, "Master, I knew you to be a hard
man, reaping where you did not sow and gathering
where you scattered no seed. And I was afraid, and
went away and hid your talent in the ground. See,
you have what is yours." But his master answered
and said to him, "You wicked, lazy slave, you knew
that I reap where I did not sow and gather where I
scattered no seed. Then you ought to have put my
money in the bank, and on my arrival I would
have received my money back with interest.
Therefore take away the talent from him, and give

it to the one who has the ten talents."
For to everyone who has, more shall be given, and
he will have an abundance; but from the one who
does not have, even what he does have shall be
taken away. Throw out the worthless slave into the
outer darkness; in that place there will be weeping
and gnashing of teeth.

Matthew 25:14-30 (NASB)

Stewards are required to take risks

It's interesting to me how upset the master got with the steward who took no risks. The other two stewards did take risks and reaped the rewards. I often wonder why the parable didn't contain a steward who lost some of the investment. But either way, I think we're led to believe that the primary frustration of the master was that the steward was lazy and didn't even try.

He was called a "wicked and lazy slave." My take on this is that he was more frustrated with his laziness than his lack of production. The steward didn't even put the talents in the bank to gain interest. The passage states that the master gave to each of them according to their ability. So, I think we can assume that the steward with one talent did have some ability, or else he wouldn't have given him any.

If he did indeed have some ability to manage money, even with the smallest amount of ability he would have known that earning small interest at the bank is better than burying it!

I liken this to having a vet watch your dog for the weekend and not feed it. Almost everyone knows you should feed a dog at least daily, but especially a vet. It's his profession, the thing he's skilled at doing and entrusted to do.

So, the extreme amount of laziness this steward had to not put the talent in the bank, coupled with the fact that he let fear paralyze him from doing what he was expected to do infuriated the master.

The parable is speaking of money, but this can also be applied to the gifts and skills that God has entrusted us with. If I refuse to step out in a gift or skill that God has given me because I'm afraid or lazy, I may be behaving the same way as the steward with one talent.

"...From everyone who has been given much, much will be required; and to whom they entrusted much, of him they will ask all the more."

Don't compare yourself to others

The master in the parable didn't give each steward the same amount. They all started with different amounts, not much different from this game of life we're all in. Some people start with a lot, some with a little. But we're all judged based on what we did with what we had, rather than what we ended up with.

The great thing about this is that our success is not based on what people may think about us. God knows what He gave us to work with, and He will see what we do with it. So, it doesn't matter whether other people think you're a success or a failure. **God's definition of success is often quite different from man's.**

The master gave them each "according to their ability." He knew a bit about their faithfulness and how likely they were to increase their talents. Turns out he delegated wisely.

Our money is not our own

We enter into the world with nothing, and we leave with nothing.

One of the first lessons I learned a few years ago that really changed the way I thought about money was that none of it is mine. It's all God's. I have the privilege and opportunity to be a steward of what He gave me.

Once I began looking at my money this way, it changed my whole financial outlook and helped me to grow more focused on pleasing God with the money entrusted to me.

Even if we spent our lives and ignored our responsibility as stewards, we still can't take any of it with us. We might as well try to better the lives of those around us and store up treasure in heaven rather than here.

DAY 3

He Cares for the Birds

"God gives every bird its food, but He doesn't throw it in the nest."

-J.G. Holland

There's a fine line between waiting on God and trying to make something happen with our own strength.

Unless the LORD builds the house,
They labor in vain who build it;
Unless the LORD guards the city,
The watchman keeps awake in vain.

Psalm 127:1 (NASB)

So, we can do some things with our own strength, but it won't be of much value. However, if "the

Lord builds the house," He'll build a nice one, a much better one than what we could produce.

Clearly, we have a part to play. I like this J.G. Holland quote because it's just a friendly reminder that God does provide, but it comes through action on our part.

He gives to the beast its food,
and to the young ravens which cry.

Psalm 147:9 (NASB)

DAY 4

Trusting God in the Midst of Bad Circumstances

I finally realized something that seems really obvious, but for some reason it took me a while to get it.

We should be just as confident that things are going to work out when they look crazy as when everything looks fine and dandy.

The opposite is true, as well. Even though things look peaceful and calm, it isn't an indication of security. **Our security comes from God.** It isn't at all dependent on what is going on around us. Whether it's the economy, our finances, our children, our marriages, we can (and should) trust God with all of it.

And we know that God causes all things to work together for good to those who love God, to those who are called according to His purpose.

Romans 8:28 (KJV)

It just dawned on me recently after going through a faith test that it really doesn't matter whether it's easy or difficult to trust God. As my circumstances began to "look" better, I noticed myself trusting a bit less in God and a bit more in myself. After all, my circumstances weren't requiring as much faith. I kind of slapped myself a bit and realized I'm no less dependent on God when things are going well as I am when they're going terribly.

The good circumstances are only an illusion of security.

When things look good, it's easy to understand how things will all work out. But isn't it amazing how quickly I can go running back to God in faith when things look bad again? I quickly realized that "good circumstances" provide no true security

The great news is that for believers, bad

circumstances are only an illusion of a *lack of security.*

Trust God in the storm

It reminds me of Jesus sleeping on the boat during the middle of the storm. He said, "Let us go to the other side." But yet when things started looking bad enough, they started to doubt that would happen. The truth is, no matter how bad things looked, they were just as secure. They had God in the flesh on the boat with them! How could they really think that they wouldn't make it?

On that day, when evening came, He said to them, "Let us go over to the other side." Leaving the crowd, they took Him along with them in the boat, just as He was; and other boats were with Him. And there arose a fierce gale of wind, and the waves were breaking over the boat so much that the boat was already filling up. Jesus Himself was in the stern, asleep on the cushion; and they woke Him and said to Him, "Teacher, do You not care that we are perishing?" And He got up and rebuked the wind and said to the sea, "Hush, be still." And the wind died down and it became perfectly calm. And He said to them, "Why are you afraid? Do you still have no faith?" They became very much afraid and said to one another, "Who then is this, that even the wind and the sea obey Him?"

Mark 4:35-41 (NASB)

When they finally were freaking out enough, they woke Him up and frustrated with their lack of faith, He told the storm to calm down. They just didn't get it. They didn't realize who Jesus was. They didn't realize that it didn't matter how bad it got, He was there with them.

It's no different for us today. We have the promise of God that He will never leave us, nor forsake us. It doesn't matter how bad things look, it's merely an illusion. Don't be deceived: when your trust is in God, you could not be more secure.

DAY 5

The Bible and Debt

Before you begin your journey to get out of debt, it's important to know what the Bible says about debt. You can then use these truths to build your faith since faith comes by hearing the Word. Once you have a solid understanding of what God has to say about the issue, then you can boldly pray about your debt in faith.

What does the Bible say about debt?

The borrower is slave to the lender. When you are in debt to another, you enter into a slave/master relationship with your creditor. (Proverbs 22:7)

God wants us to lend to others. Obviously, this is difficult if you don't have anything to lend.

(Deuteronomy 15:6, 28:12, Matthew 5:42)

We are required to pay back what we borrowed. It is easy to take this lightly, but if we borrowed it, we should pay it back. (Psalm 37:21, Ecclesiastes 5:4).

What the Bible does NOT say about debt?

That it is a sin to be in debt. As mentioned above, it isn't God's best for us, but the Bible does not say that it's a sin.

What are the Biblical promises about debt?

The way I look at it, Jesus came to set us free from the bondage of sin. We were slaves to sin until He set us free. If He wanted to set us free in one area, why would He want us to be slaves in another?

I also love Deuteronomy 28:12:

The Lord will open for you His good storehouse, the heavens, to give rain to your land in its season and to bless all the work of your hand; and you shall lend to many nations, but you shall not borrow.

This verse is one of the promises that I stand on when praying about my debt. The prerequisite listed in Deuteronomy 28:1 is that we "diligently obey the Lord your God."

God can NOT keep us out of debt

I believe God would love to see His children living debt-free lives. But, as stewards of the money that He has entrusted to us we have a free will to do what we wish with it. We can choose to give it, save it, spend it or even spend more than we have.

I also believe God will work on our behalf to help get us out of debt, but we have a big part to play – to stop spending more than we have! It doesn't matter how much God provides – **as long as we are spending more money than we have, we will always be in debt.**

It's bigger than us

As Christians we have the opportunity to use our finances to build God's Kingdom. Every decision we make about our money may be much larger than we realize.

Speaking for myself, I know it's easy to get caught up in trying to store up treasures on earth, when I know I should be storing them up in heaven. Every time I do, I get a gentle nudge back on to the narrow path that I'm so thankful for. Storing up treasures in heaven is the way to live!

DAY 6

Would Jesus Have an Emergency Fund?

I talk a lot about the importance of having an emergency fund and how it's a necessary ingredient to a sound financial plan. But, I thought we should step back and ask the necessary question, "Would Jesus have an emergency fund?"

In trying to answer this question, the first verse that came to mind was *Proverbs 27:12 (NLT)*

A prudent person foresees danger and takes precautions. The simpleton goes blindly on and suffers the consequences.

The whole purpose of having an emergency fund is to prepare for when the inevitable "trials of life" hit. Christians are not exempt these trials and struggles that seem to pop up unexpectedly.

This reminds me of the parable of the foolish virgins in Matthew 25:1-13. From what I can tell, the **foolish** virgins brought enough oil for their lamps had the bridegroom showed up on time. Well, the bridegroom was probably playing football with some friends and showed up a little late. (And he didn't even call to say he was going to be late!)

What separated the foolish from the wise was their preparation for the unexpected. The virgins forever known as foolish, didn't plan for the unexpected by bringing extra oil. Those who were labeled wise brought extra oil in preparation for the unexpected.

Jesus knew the balance of what part He played and what He should rely on God to do. We have a part to play, but it's foolish of us to think higher of ourselves than we ought and think we have a more important role than we actually do. Ultimately, God is the one who supplies all of our needs (see Philippians 4:19).
But Jesus also said:

Do not store up for yourselves treasures on earth,

*where moth and rust destroy, and where thieves
break in and steal. But store up for yourselves
treasures in heaven, where neither moth nor rust
destroys, and where thieves do not break in or
steal; for where your treasure is, there your heart
will be also.*

Matthew 6:19-21 (ESV)

I get convicted by this verse when I have a
temptation to think that if I can save enough
money, I can insulate myself from any and all
problems, thus not needing God. I have to fight
against the tendency to trust in myself and depend
on my abilities rather than God's.

The truth is that we can never make enough smart
financial decisions or do enough things right that
we will not need Him. He designed it that way. We
are imperfect beings who are dependent on God.

So, as far as Jesus' emergency fund goes, if He
were walking the earth today, I think He would
have one, but He would still trust God for His daily
bread (see Matthew 6:11).

DAY 7

Camels and Needles

Have you ever tried to squeeze a camel through the eye of a needle?

Ah, you know the verse. It's the one people love to quote when they're trying to prove that Christians should be poor because it appears more righteous. Well, is it really?

For it is easier for a camel to go through the eye of a needle than for a rich man to enter the kingdom of God.

Luke 18:25 (NASB)

Let's look at the definition of "rich" and see who qualifies.

According to Webster's Dictionary:

*Rich = having abundant possessions and
especially material wealth*

Why doesn't it tell me how much money I need to have to actually be rich?

In fact, I looked the definition up in seven different dictionaries and not one gives a specific definition of rich. None of them offer a specific annual income to indicate whether you're rich or not. Hmmm... So how can we know who's rich and who isn't? Where is the line drawn?

Is it the top 10 percent wealthiest people? The top 5 percent or 1 percent?

Well, if you make $15,000 per year you're richer than 90 percent of the world. If you make $25,000 per year you are in the top 2 percent. And if you make $40,000 you are in the top 1 percent of the richest people in the world. (Check for yourself at globalrichlist.com.)

So, how do you define rich?

Are you wealthier than you realized?

The verse can really strike fear into the hearts of people causing them to run from money. But the truth is that money isn't the issue. It's a matter of the heart. If we understand that the money isn't ours, but that it's actually God's and we're merely its stewards, then it's easier not to depend on it.

People who realize they're stewards cannot be rich, because they know it isn't their money.

Won't I be safe if I never have a lot of money?

Many people have taken this verse to think that by not having much, they're safe. By lying back and not really working hard, you can rest assured you will never have much money come into your hands, so therefore you can't be rich as the verse mentions.

Personally, I think Jesus addressed this in the parable of the talents. The steward to whom he gave one talent did nothing with it except bury it. The master called him wicked and lazy. To me that rules out the possibility that just being lazy and not earning money will make you righteous.

One of my readers noted:

"The amount of money that we have is irrelevant. We are all meant to live abundantly. The problem arises when your love for money supersedes your love for God. Jesus is pointing out that it is easy for a person with lots of money to become attached to the money and therefore makes it hard to give that up for God. i.e. Love for God above all else. Of course this can happen for anyone with any amount of money."

And another reader added:

"I agree with the commenter above who thinks this is about the person's attitude. It's hard for a rich person to enter the kingdom of heaven because he usually has other things on his mind, namely his wealth (protecting it, growing it, enjoying it), and puts it before everything else. As such, serving God and living according to Jesus' teachings is far, far removed from his thoughts and actions."

Personally, I think the comments above are right on target.

As mentioned above, I don't think an actual dollar amount defines "rich." I have seen people with not much money who would qualify as "rich" like the young man in that passage, because they're so attached to their possessions. You don't need much money (or any money for that matter) to make money a higher priority than God.

Matthew 6:24 says:

> *No one can serve two masters; for either he will hate the one and love the other, or else he will be loyal to the one and despise the other. You cannot serve God and mammon.*

On the other hand, I have seen people who had a ton of cash but realized they were merely stewards of what God had given them and cared very little about material possessions. They were focused on using their wealth to help people and do whatever God required of them. They gladly gave their money, because they were not serving money but were serving God.

So what do you do?

Stop serving money. The Bible says you cannot serve God and money. (See Matt 6:24.) You have to pick. We will either make decisions based on our walk with God or based on how they will affect us financially. Should you take that job? "Of course, it pays more," is not the correct response. Our decisions should not be made solely on their impact on our wallets.

Be content. It doesn't matter whether we have a lot or a little. We're called to be content with what we have. The apostle Paul talked about how he learned how to be content whether he was in a dungeon or living in the king's palace. He understood contentment.

Don't be afraid of money. It is the LOVE of money that's the root of all evil. (1 Timothy 6:10) Not money itself. If that were the case, then nothing good could come out of it. But every day God's purposes and plans are coming to pass via the use of money.

Give. Giving is a tangible way to break any attachment to money. If you don't want to give, that's probably a good indication that you *need* to give.

DAY 8

It's ONLY Money

This is a good thing to say when faced with a financial difficulty. It's very difficult to utter those words sometimes, but it's good for us to do so. This isn't an excuse to be lackadaisical with our money, but it is an acknowledgement that there's **so much more to life** than money.

I am all for being a great steward of the resources and finances that God has provided, but when it comes down to it, He is the one who meets our needs! (see Philippians 4:19.) And last time I read the verse, there weren't any prerequisites like being extremely organized, being really disciplined, managing money like a pro or even not making mistakes. Even with all our imperfections and "human-ness," the Bible still says that He will provide all our needs according to His riches and glory.

So, as difficult as it may seem, next time a financial difficulty arises, push out those three words, "It's only money." Just by saying this, you minimize its importance in your life. Money is not supposed to the primary focus (aka lord) of our lives.

As I'm writing, I'm thinking back to a few difficult times during the past few years when I needed my wonderful wife to help me make that confession. Whether it's easy to say or not, IT IS TRUE. Money comes and money goes. It's ONLY money. Don't worry about it, just keep trusting God. He's the one who takes care of you.

Look at the birds of the air, that they do not sow, nor reap nor gather into barns, and yet your heavenly Father feeds them. Are you not worth much more than they?

Matthew 6:26 (NASB)

DAY 9

Tithing in the New Testament

As long as I have been a Christian, I can remember people arguing and debating about tithing. Some say it was only an Old Testament law that doesn't need to be followed as believers of the New Covenant. And some say that it's just a relevant to New Testament Christians as it was in the Old Covenant.

I recently wrote about my tithing experience and I'd like to offer my thoughts on tithing.

It isn't a means of salvation

You can't earn your way to Heaven by your tithing.

For it is by grace you have been saved, through faith–and this not from yourselves, it is the gift of God– not by works, so that no one can boast.

Ephesians 2:8-9 (NIV)

Out of our faith our good works manifest. So, in my opinion, if someone truly understands how great a gift they have received, they will expend a lot of energy giving back.

Can you be blessed without tithing?

Some say you won't be blessed if you don't tithe. I kind of think this depends on the person and their maturity level as a Christian. You expect more from a 13-year-old than a five-year-old, right? I don't think God is any different, He knows where we are on our walk and will meet us where we are.

I was a Christian for a while before I started tithing, and I think I was doing okay. I know some Christians who don't tithe and seem to be very blessed. But, I don't really think there is any getting around the fact that you will be MORE blessed if you tithe, than if you don't. And to be honest, giving 10 percent should just be a mile marker on our giving journey. If we truly understand how much we have received, we will spend our whole lives trying to give way beyond 10 percent.

The Bible says there will ALWAYS be seedtime and harvest (Genesis 8:22). What we sow, we will reap. If we give, we will receive in good measure. So the bottom line is that there's undoubtedly a blessing that comes to givers.

Give, and it will be given to you. A good measure, pressed down, shaken together and running over, will be poured into your lap. For with the measure you use, it will be measured to you.

Luke 6:38 (NIV)

God loves a cheerful giver

Each man should give what he has decided in his heart to give, not reluctantly or under compulsion, for God loves a cheerful giver.

2 Corinthians 9:7 (NIV)

God loves a cheerful giver, not under compulsion. If you aren't giving with the right attitude, don't waste your time. If you have a bad attitude about it and want to change it, just ask God for help. He will.

Tithing verses in the New Testament

There are a ton of verses about tithing in the Old Testament and a lot fewer in the New Testament. It is true that tithing isn't talked about nearly as much in the New Testament as the Old Testament. Personally, I don't believe that in any way nullifies the value of it as a practice.

Under the New Covenant our salvation is not based upon our obedience to the 10 Commandments, but does that mean we shouldn't still follow them? Are they suddenly of no value? I think the same can be said of tithing.

While you can debate all day long about whether or not it's a command for New Testament believers, it will still provide a blessing just as it did in the Old Covenant.

A fellow blogger brought up two great points about New Testament tithing.

1. Jesus endorsed the tithe

In Matthew 23:23 and Luke 11:42 Jesus referred to tithing as something that <u>should not be neglected</u>.

Woe to you, teachers of the law and Pharisees, you hypocrites! You give a tenth of your spices - mint, dill and cummin. But you have neglected the more important matters of the law - justice, mercy and faithfulness. You should have practiced the latter, without neglecting the former.

2. As New Testament believers we answer to a higher calling

Like it or not, we're living under the New Covenant, and as a result, we have increased responsibilities in certain areas.

...From everyone who has been given much, much will be demanded; and from the one who has been entrusted with much, much more will be asked.

Luke 12:48 (NIV)

From my <u>blogger friend</u>

"No longer are animal sacrifices necessary, but we are now to sacrifice our own lives and live for

Christ, not ourselves. No longer is 'an eye for an eye' appropriate but we are to love our enemies and 'turn the other cheek.' These are only two examples of heightened responsibilities Jesus taught His people. As such, I can only conclude that the same holds true with the tithe. While it used to be the requirement, it should now be the minimum."

He said we could test Him

Do we have any better invitation that to actually test it out and see whether it really works? Most of us who do tithe were probably in the same spot as the non-tithers and didn't believe it ourselves, but we tried it out. Guess what, just like God promised, things are better after tithing!

It really is like all the other areas of our walk with God – it requires FAITH. No it doesn't make sense that when we give all this money away, things will actually be better, but I have found it true in my own life and many other readers have, as well.

"Bring the whole tithe into the storehouse, that there may be food in my house. Test me in this," says the LORD Almighty, "and see if I will not throw open the floodgates of heaven and pour out so much blessing that you will not have room

enough for it."

Malachi 3:10 (NIV)

It is so much bigger than us

The much bigger issue here is that God's Kingdom needs to be advanced!

Who does He use to do that? Us, the believers! If we aren't funding and financing Kingdom activities, then who will? How are the lost going to be reached if we don't send those to preach? (Romans 10:15)

We shouldn't get all caught up in percentages and what we "have to do" according to the Bible – what we (as God's people) need to do is to forget about our ambitions, goals and motives and pick up God's plan.

The grace of God saved us from eternal separation from Him! With all that we have received, how can we do anything else but give all we have?

What if we all got our minds off our own earthly bank accounts and focused on sowing into things that will have eternal value.

*"I judge all things only by the price
they shall gain in eternity."*

- John Wesley

I know it's difficult to comprehend, but eternity is
a LONG TIME! We can either do things with our
time and money that may benefit us for a few years
here on earth, or we can see ourselves as the
eternal beings that we are, get our priorities lined
up with God's and starting giving in a way that will
actually last for eternity!

*But store up for yourselves treasures in heaven,
where moth and rust do not destroy, and where
thieves do not break in and steal.*

Matthew 6:20 (NIV)

When we give to our churches and to ministries
that are reaching the world, we get to be included
in their eternal reward. We are the BODY of Christ;
we all have a part to play.

*...from whom the whole body, being fitted and
held together by what every joint supplies,
according to the proper working of each
individual part, causes the growth of the body for
the building up of itself in love.*

Ephesians 4:16

The amazing thing is that as we start getting our focus off ourselves and on meeting the needs of others, we will have our needs taken care of. It's just the way God set it up. He's so good, isn't He?

DAY 10

Stewardship: What Is It Really?

Stewardship is something I hear a lot of talk about, but not a lot of understanding. I truly believe that understanding what stewardship is and how it applies to our lives will change the way we make decisions each day.

If we really understand what it means to be good stewards, we will begin to not only see our lives change, but also the world around us. Like all other Biblical principles, we gain tremendous benefit by following them.

The definition of stewardship

Let's look at the actual definition of stewardship.

Stewardship:

1: the office, duties, and obligations of a steward

2: the conducting, supervising, or managing of something; especially: the careful and responsible management of something entrusted to one's care <stewardship of our natural resources>

I like how it says "managing of something." To me this implies we have decisions to make and are responsible for what we're stewards over. Just like a manager of a business is responsible for his/her department and employees, so are we with all that's entrusted to us.

So do we actually steward?

Personally, I believe it applies to everything we have. Our time, our money, our God-given gifts and abilities, our influence, it all comes from God. There are lots of stewardship verses that show us how we should act, but my favorite is the Parable of the Talents since it gives such a great illustration of what a good steward does.

Put simply, the good stewards were the ones who took **"risks" and action** in order to multiply what God gave them. The bad steward was the one who out of fear decided not to take a risk and was called lazy as well.

This reminds me of another scripture.

From everyone who has been given much, much will be demanded; and from the one who has been entrusted with much, much more will be asked.

Luke 12:48 (NIV)

How should "stewardship living" affect our lives?

Our finances tend to be the key area that people refer to when speaking of stewardship. I think the main reason is that often money is one of the most difficult things for people to give. At least for me, that used to be the case. I was okay giving my energy, time, or sharing my abilities, but money was not something I was interested in giving away. That's probably why God had to work on me for so long to help me lose my attitude!

One of the things that helped me was keeping focused on the fact that I came into the world with nothing and will leave with nothing. I began to look at all my possessions as merely being "on loan." This has helped me begin to see myself more as a "steward" rather than a "possessor."

Stewardship of a violin

I remember a friend of mine saying that he was talking to a well-known violinist about his violin. The violinist had mentioned that the violin was a couple of hundred years old and worth many hundreds of thousands of dollars. The interesting point I remember from the conversation was the way the violinist viewed himself as a steward of the instrument. He knew that many great musicians had played the instrument before he was even born. He was also not naive to think that he would be the last to play the fine instrument. He understood that it was just temporarily passing through his hands.

The violinist's outlook on his violin has really helped me get a better understanding of the role possessions should have in my life. Changing my thinking in this way has affected how I handle my money and even my weekly buying decisions. It's not that having possessions is a good or bad thing, just that they need to be viewed in the proper perspective.

DAY 11

No One Really Wants Money

Is it really money that everyone is after?

It isn't.

> *He who loves money will not be*
> *satisfied with money...*
>
> *Ecclesiastes 5:10*

The last time I checked, we still cannot eat money, knit a sweater from it, or build a roof with it. So, a million dollars while stranded on an deserted island is about useless.

No one really wants money, but rather, **they want**

what they think it will provide. Some want to get out of debt, have a BMW, buy a yacht, feel a sense of financial security, and some want to have the prestige or power they think it brings. But the pieces of cloth and paper we call cash is ultimately not what people are interested in.

And of course, even the things that money may provide shouldn't be sought after.

But seek first his kingdom and his righteousness, and all these things will be given to you as well.

Matthew 6:33 (NIV)

DAY 12

Why God's Way Takes Longer

It's kind of like becoming a tree

I was staring at a tree the other day just day-dreaming and kind of worrying about how long it was taking to get answers to prayer for a few issues in my life. I was reminded of...

*How blessed is the man who does not walk in the counsel of the wicked, nor stand in the path of sinners, nor sit in the seat of scoffers! But his delight is in the law of the LORD, and in His law **he meditates day and night.***

*He will be **like a tree** firmly planted by streams of water, which yields its fruit **in its season** and its*

*leaf does not wither; and in **whatever he does, he
prospers.***

Psalms 1:1-3 (NASB)

In my case I have been diligently trying not to
"walk in the counsel of the wicked," and it seems to
be making my answers to prayer take even longer.
I have been earnestly trying to do things the right
way, knowing full well that by cutting a few
corners or compromising my values I could make
the answers appear faster. The major difference is
that I can get mediocre answers doing it my way or
the fruit God promises by doing it His way.

The prerequisite for our fruit bearing from Psalms
1 is that we:

- Do things God's way
- Stay in the Word

If we do these two things we have the promise that
whatever we do will prosper and that we WILL
bear fruit IN OUR SEASON.

Trees grow slowly

As I was staring at this tree I began to realize that
trees grow slowly (how is that for a revelation?).

You plant a seed for a tree and it takes a while to sprout and takes a while to grow to a decent size.

Grass and even plants, on the other hand, grow a lot faster. They sprout up quickly and sometimes you can even notice growth one day to the next. I have been enjoying watching this rapid growth with all of the plants in my vegetable garden.

Grass grows fast

Then it kind of hit me that God wants to make me "like a tree." He isn't interested in seeing rapid growth that will not make it to the next season and is ultimately unsustainable. A tree, though it grows slowly, becomes a lot more sturdy and can withstand challenges that grass and plants can't.

I'm reminded of a storm we recently had that snapped my tomato plant right in half. The plant had grown to about 2.5 feet in a matter of months and was not strong enough to survive when the winds came. God wants to make us strong and sturdy to withstand the storms in our lives.

*That when **the wicked sprouted up like grass** and all who did iniquity flourished, it was only that they might be destroyed forevermore.*

Psalms 92:7

The righteous man will flourish like the palm tree,
he will grow like a cedar in Lebanon.

Psalms 92:12

Trees yield more fruit

I'm excited about what my tomato plants will
produce this summer, but even the best tomato
plant would be lucky to produce 40 pounds of
tomatoes in a season. But mature apple trees can
produce more than 1000 pounds in a season.

The downside, of course, is that trees don't bear
fruit three months after you plant them like many
vegetable plants will. Some trees will take a few
years or even longer to bear fruit. I remember the
frustration I had with this when I wanted apples
from a new tree and learned I had to wait a while.

Patience seems to be a rare virtue in our society
these days, but it is one we ought to develop. God
seems to like taking the long road with a lot of
things, and as I begin to see the reason behind it, I
say, "Huh, God really is smarter than I am."

Trying to be a tree

It's tough watching the grass sprout up all around you and seeing others bearing fruit when you have been faithfully doing what is right, but we mustn't be short-sighted. We need to try to look at these things the way God sees them.

Though the tomato plants around us may be popping out some fruit, while we seem to wonder what's taking so long, our day will come. God is working and creating something in us that will be around long after the grass has come and gone.

*And let us not lose heart and grow weary and faint in acting nobly and doing right, for in due time and **at the appointed season** we shall reap, if we do not loosen and relax our courage and faint.*

Galatians 6:9 (AMP)

DAY 13

Financial Lessons from Solomon

The Bible says that Solomon was the richest man who ever lived and also the wisest ever to live (see 1 Kings 4:31). I think that makes him qualified to give some financial advice.

1. Money does not satisfy

He who loves money with not be satisfied with money

Ecclesiastes 5:10

Loving money is a dangerous thing. Some people spend their entire lives chasing more and more money thinking that it will bring them satisfaction, only to never actually attain the satisfaction they were searching for.

2. True satisfaction only comes from God.

It doesn't come from getting married, a bigger house, a mil in the bank, or being retired. What is interesting is that when we take our focus off getting more money and more things, then they seem to start appearing. I guess this is what was meant by the verse in Matthew,

But seek <u>first</u> His kingdom and His righteousness, and all these things will be added to you.

Matthew 6:33 (NASB)

3. Diversify your investments

Divide your portion to seven, or even to eight, for you do not know what misfortune may occur on the earth.

Ecclesiastes 11:2

I get two things out of this verse. First, that Solomon lays out the groundwork for diversification. I like the balance of having seven to eight "eggs in the basket," rather than just one that would leave us with nothing if it turned out rotten.

But also, 200 minuscule eggs are worth next to nothing individually. In this case, if any one investment performed very well, it would make very little impact on the portfolio as a whole. On the other hand, if you had seven investments and any one of them performed well, it would have a decent impact on the portfolio as a whole.

4. There's never a perfect time

He who watches the wind will not sow and he who looks at the clouds will not reap.

Ecclesiastes 11:4

I think the reason that some of us wait for the perfect time to do something is because we're trying to wait until there's no risk. It's human nature; we want to eliminate any and all risk of bad things happening. No matter how much we try, we can NEVER eliminate all risk. Any time we step out into anything there's some level of risk, but that's not an excuse not to take action.

If it's stepping out into a new job, taking the first step to get out of debt, quit a bad habit, or anything else, there's always an excuse not to take action. Step out and be one of those people who realizes that the perfect time is now.

5. Work smarter, not harder

If the axe is dull and he does not sharpen its edge, then he must exert more strength...

Ecclesiastes 10:10

Steven Covey calls this his seventh habit of i effective people. He calls it "Sharpening the Saw." Sometimes the most effective thing we can do is to rest. Though, it seems counterintuitive, it really isn't. Resting, allows for more production during your productive hours. People who live by this principle realize that often six hours can be more productive when accompanied with rest than 10 without.

This was another lesson I learned the hard way while in school. I would frequently spend four hours on homework, when I'm sure I could have done it easily in two hours. I was living in a sleep-deprived, zombie-like state because I "had better things to do with my time than sleep." But because my brain was functioning well below its capability, it took me a lot longer to finish my assignments.

My best success with this is to regularly ask myself whether I'm working hard or working smart. They aren't mutually exclusive, but if you're only focusing on working hard without actually thinking about whether it's the smartest method, then you could be wasting your time with a dull axe.

DAY 14

Why I Think You Should Set a Goal

A few years ago I started meeting with a "life coach" (my term, not his) who I was looking for some guidance from on how to succeed in a few particular areas of my life. He was a very wealthy, successful, God-fearing guy who just seemed to have it all together. He was a friend of a friend, and I jumped at the chance to meet with him – hoping to glean something from him to help me in some of the more frustrating areas of my life.

One of those areas was my career. While it appeared that there were tremendous career opportunities within reach, there was an invisible barrier that I just could not seem to get past.

After spending year after year trying and failing, I began to lose hope. What was so frustrating to me was that I knew I had certain gifts and skill sets, but in the job I had, they were completely unnecessary and even looked down upon.

Looking back on the whole experience, it's clear to me that God actually spared me because had I gotten one of the promotions I wanted, I likely wouldn't have had the motivation to take the leap to start my own business. It was the desperation and the thought of having to spend another 20 to 30 years in a job I hated that made it pretty easy to embrace the "risk" of starting my own business.

Anyway, back to the life coach...

We first met at a Cheesecake Factory, and I remember walking in and almost immediately after shaking his hand, he said rather bluntly, "So, what do you want?" I had thought about a lot of things I didn't want in life, a low-paying job, a job I hated, a dead-end career path, were all at the top of my list, but I hadn't really spent much time thinking about things I wanted. He made me.

Once I could decide on specific things that I wanted in life (particularly in the next five years) he had me write them down. This list is what became my five-year goals.

At the time I wrote them, I knew that God could do anything. I mean, looking at the transformation that took place in Joseph's life, I knew that God could help me to reach those goals, but it seemed as if it would be the same caliber of miracle as it was for Joseph.

It's a weird feeling writing down goals that you have no possible idea of how they can ever manifest in your life. Part of the challenge for me was my fear of failure. It was easier for me NOT to set a goal, because that I way I would avoid any failures.

I knew this wasn't the way I should live my life, but I was doing it anyway. Looking back, I realize that I kind of lived the opposite of a life of faith – if I couldn't see it or at least figure out how it was possible, I didn't truly believe that it was possible.

Three years later

I just had a conversation with my old life coach the other day, and it dawned on me that almost all of the goals I wrote down had come to pass – and I have lots of reasons to believe that all of them will come to pass by the five-year mark.

Remembering what I was thinking at the time is what amazes me about this. From my vantage point, the goals I wrote seemed equally as unlikely as if I had written that I wanted to walk on Mars or become the president of the U.S.

Where is God in all this?

Now, I know without a shadow of a doubt that it was the Lord. I expended all of my energy and know-how trying to reach some of these goals on my own – to no avail. I know that while I had a part in all of this, by being diligent, working hard, etc., I could have never reached these goals on my own.

For most of my Christian life, I was somewhat hesitant about goal-setting because I didn't want to get caught up in "my plans" rather than God's plans. I always wanted to do His will over my own and never wanted to get caught up in just doing a bunch of "works" for God that weren't what He had in mind for me.

But what I think happened was that even though I was writing those goals from my own interests and desires, they were actually God's plans for me. John 15:7 says,

If you abide in Me, and My words abide in you, ask whatever you wish, and it will be done for you.

Looking at that verse, we can see that this whole writing-goals-down thing isn't a formula that we can use to manipulate God. It starts with us abiding in Him and getting in the Bible so that our wills better align with His. And apparently, as that happens, the natural result is that the things we ask have a better chance of being in line with His will.

Even still, I don't assume that any goals I set are automatically God's will, but now when I set goals, I prayerfully seek after them submitting to whatever God has in mind.

The role of faith

Hebrews 11:6 says that without faith it's impossible to please God. That is a big and bold statement. I interpret it like this: **if I want to please God, I need to believe in something that I can't figure out how it will happen.**

As I mentioned before, when I was writing that original set of goals I knew that I could not reach them on my own. I had tried and failed. Again and again. I knew that the only way I would reach them was if God was at work behind the scenes.

Personally, I didn't at all feel as if I had the faith to believe they could happen. But it seems to me that the act of just writing the goals down and opening up to the possibility of failure was a huge step of faith - perhaps just a mustard-seed sized amount - but faith nonetheless that God honored.

If you haven't already, give it a try

I have a feeling that God has some remarkable things He wants to do in our lives, and He is just waiting for us to believe they're possible. If you have some desires, dreams, or things that you long to see changed in your life or in the world around you, I encourage you to write them down. Make a list of how you would like your world to be different five years from now.

Don't worry about the "how." Our job isn't to figure out how everything will happen, rather it's to trust that God knows how to make it happen. Once you have your list, don't stop there. Put it on your desk, fridge, or by your bed. Pray about the things listed and be honest with God. Look at it often and think about the things on your list.

When our minds are confronted with a question, they seek an answer. Ask yourself how you can take the first step toward reaching this goal.

What is one single thing you can do today to reach this goal?

Continue to keep the goals in the forefront of your mind, and you might just be surprised to see where you are in a few years.

DAY 15

What Really Stands Out to Me from Jesus Feeding 5000

I just read John 6 today, and the same verse stuck out to me that usually does. It's a verse that doesn't really seem as if it should make sense, but for that reason, just the fact that Jesus said it makes it all the more important for us to understand and live by. I don't think I have ever heard a preacher talk about the verse, even though I have heard this story mentioned many times since it's one of the more famous ones.

The verse was the first thing Jesus said after he performed a miracle and fed 5000 from two fish and five loaves. So Jesus took the loaves and fish and turned it into thousands of loaves and fishes to feed all these people - without even breaking a sweat. It was not difficult for Jesus to accomplish, and if it was anything like some of his other miracles it may have been as simple as His believing and speaking it into existence.

But as seemingly simple as it was to feed these 5000 people, after they ate He immediately told the disciples to:

> "Gather up the leftover fragments that nothing may be lost"
>
> John 6:12 (NASB)

What's so interesting to me is that if I had a party and fed 5000 people, I would expect there to be a lot of leftover food. I would probably try to save some of it, but realistically I would expect there to be a lot that would go to waste, and I would just figure that to be appropriate given the size of the group.

Even if I had personally spent three days preparing food for the people and invested dozens of hours of my precious time into it, I would still be okay with some waste just thinking it comes with the territory of feeding all these people.

But Jesus treated this situation completely differently. He didn't spend any time (from what we can tell) preparing it. If he had spent three days preparing it, it might make a little more sense if He said something like, "I just spent three days and thousands of dollars to get this food for you, therefore I don't want any of it to go to waste.

But instead, it was more like the bread continued to pour out of a never-ending basket.
Even though waste should have been expected (for a crowd of 5000) He made sure there wasn't any.

If I were one of the disciples I probably would have thought to myself, "Why are we picking up these scraps? He just created thousands of loaves and fishes out of thin air; do we really need the leftovers?"

Clearly, the Lord was trying to make a point.

My takeaway

As an American, I am part of a society that, because we are rich, we waste a lot of stuff. In fact, 1.3 BILLION tons of food get wasted each year. And what I have noticed in my own life is that when I have more, I care less about wasting stuff.

In my own life, I try to, regardless of how things are going financially, keep this verse in mind. It's a bit easier when money is tight, but when things are going better it can be really difficult to care about the "small change." But clearly the Lord wants us to minimize waste whether we have to work hard for the excess or whether it comes easily.

Keeping things balanced

It can be easy to take a verse like this and go to the extreme, but I really do believe that keeping it in balance is key. On the other end of the spectrum, in Matthew 26:6-10 we see Jesus defending what the disciples view as waste with the woman with the alabaster jar. In this passage, Jesus defends the woman and says that what she is doing is "beautiful." So, it seems to me that there are appropriate times to splurge and appropriate times to save.

DAY 16

It Is More Blessed to Give Than to Receive

Philippians has always been one of my favorite books of the Bible, and I have always had a particular fondness for the fourth chapter. It's one of the most joyous books in the Bible and even though we might expect that it was written during wonderfully joyous circumstances, it was actually written while Paul was in prison.

Add to that the fact that Paul was imprisoned unjustly and that a Roman prison would make an American prison look like a country club, and it proves that there must have been something to what he was writing.

Anyway, in Philippians 4:17 [AMP] Paul says this

to the Philippian church...

Not that I seek or am eager for [your] gift, but I do seek and am eager for the fruit which increases to your credit. [the harvest of blessing that is accumulating to your account]

When reading this verse yesterday, I was reminded of the blessing that comes from giving. It's a wonderful thing to give out of discipline and obedience, but sometimes we need to be reminded there's a blessing that comes as a result of our giving!

It is better to give than to receive!

Apparently, Paul learned this from Jesus.

*In everything I did, I showed you that by this kind of hard work we must help the weak, remembering the words the Lord Jesus himself said: "**It is more blessed to give than to receive.**"*

Acts 20:35 (NIV)

And I love how the amplified version adds a little more detail about what it means to be blessed.

...It is more blessed (makes one happier and

more to be envied) to give than to receive.

Acts 20:35 (AMP)

Maybe I just needed a little encouragement in this area, but I was blessed by this reminder that God has a "blessing account" for us that is accumulating as we give!

DAY 17

12 Great Giving Quotes to Ponder

Today, I figured it might be good for us to get inspired with some great giving quotes. These are some of the favorites I've found so far.

"No person was ever honored for what he received. He was honored for what he gave."

— Calvin Coolidge

"The value of a man resides in what he gives and not in what he is capable of receiving."

— Albert Einstein

"Make all you can, save all you can, give all you can."

— John Wesley

"It is possible to give without loving, but it is impossible to love without giving."

— Richard Braunstein

"He who obtains has little. He who scatters has much."

— Lao-Tzu

"You can't have a perfect day without doing something for someone who'll never be able to repay you."

— John Wooden

"You can have everything in life that you want if you will just help enough other people get what they want."

— Zig Ziglar

"If a person gets his attitude toward money straight, it will help straighten out almost every other
area in his life."

– Billy Graham

"Remember this–you can't serve God and Money, but you can serve God with money."

– Selwyn Hughes

"I judge all things only by the price they shall gain in eternity."

– John Wesley

"As base a thing as money often is, yet it can be transmuted into everlasting treasure. It can be converted into food for the hungry and clothing for the poor. It can keep a missionary actively winning lost men to the light of the gospel and thus transmute itself into heavenly values. Any temporal possession can be turned into everlasting wealth. Whatever is given to Christ is immediately touched with immortality."

— A.W. Tozer

"It is more blessed to give than to receive."

— Jesus, in Acts 20:35

DAY 18

Being Owed Money and Striving to Pass the Test

I once heard someone say, "Challenges are just wonderfully disguised opportunities for growth." I really do believe it's true. Just like a strong physical body requires exercises that push it beyond what's comfortable, so a strong character requires challenges that aren't comfortable.

My newest challenge is that an advertiser owes me a lot of money.

The first time someone owed me money

I remember as a teen selling my guitar to an acquaintance from church and after months of reminders and little to no payments I realized I wasn't likely to ever receive full payment for the guitar.

As a fairly young Christian, I learned two lessons.

First, that Christians are people just like everyone else who make mistakes and don't always do what they should.

Second, that I could "fight for my right" in the flesh, or I could let God vindicate me.

At that point in my life, the $400 he owed me was a huge sum of money, and it was honestly very difficult to place that concern on the Lord. I prayed about it for weeks, and it became clear that the best course of action was to deliberately SOW the guitar into his life.

I realized I could either have a victim mentality, thinking that something was stolen from me, or I could choose that he didn't steal it, but I GAVE it, knowing that the Lord sees my heart and would reward that.

Looking back on this lesson, as difficult as it was, I

knew it was good for my character development. It helped me take a great step forward in breaking any love of money that was present in my life and ultimately helped me to learn better to put my trust in God rather than trying to make things happen myself.

Give to everyone who asks of you, and whoever takes away what is yours, do not demand it back.

Luke 6:30 (NASB)

A new challenge

Fast forward a few years, and I have a new opportunity for growth. With my job (running SeedTime.com), I receive payments from quite a few different advertisers and ad networks. Up until recently, I was making the mistake of not thoroughly keeping track of my payments. I just assumed that if they owed me money, they would just pay me.

As a result of my naiveté, one particular advertiser went months without paying and owed me many times more than what I was owed for the guitar. At first I just contacted the company to let it know, assuming it was just a mistake and that it would just pay off the remaining balance. Instead, the last couple of months I've called and emailed a lot getting little to no response and even less in payments.

As if the large chunk of change the company owes me weren't enough, this is money I pay my bills with. It seems that the stakes are quite a bit higher than they were with the guitar in high school.

At the peak of my frustration I stumbled upon this verse...

Let your forbearing spirit be known to all men.

Philippians 4:5 (NASB)

And just guess what the definition of "forbearing" is.

Webster's defines it as, "a refraining from the enforcement of something (as a debt, right, or obligation) that is due."

I think God was trying to make a point to me, and He laid it on so thick, I finally got it. To add to that, I felt as if I were supposed to apologize to the advertiser for being too overbearing. After arguing and coming up with about 100 reasons the company should apologize to me, rather than the other way around, I obeyed and sent an email apologizing for my behavior.

The next verse in Philippians 4 says...

Be anxious for nothing, but in everything by prayer and supplication with thanksgiving let your requests be made known to God.

Philippians 4:6

While all this was going on, we were saving up every dime we could find so we could come up with the required down payment for our first house. I have to admit it was difficult not being anxious knowing that if this company would just send what it owed, we would comfortably have our down payment covered. I guess that was part of the test.

So after all that, I convinced myself to put it in the Lord's hands and allow Him to work on the situation.

It's all a test

There are some good practical business lessons I've learned from all this that will serve me well in the future, but much more valuable are the lessons

God is teaching me about my character and how to do things His way.

This advertiser will probably never pay me, but I'm confident that obeying God's Word will always yield the best result - even if I don't see it right away.

DAY 19

Seek First the Kingdom of God and Then...

I was reading in Jeremiah this morning and stumbled on this verse...

For the shepherds have become stupid and have not sought the LORD; therefore they have not prospered, and all their flock is scattered.

Jeremiah 10:21 (NASB)

It kind of hit me, because I have had times of feeling guilty like those shepherds – times where I got too caught up in doing my own thing to seek God.

It's interesting to me that not only does it say they didn't prosper, but their flock was scattered, as well. I would equate that in today's terms to having chaos at our jobs, in our finances, or in other areas of our lives.

Benefits of seeking first the Kingdom

The encouraging news is that as we seek after God, good things follow.

Keep the charge of the LORD your God, to walk in His ways, to keep His statutes, His commandments, His ordinances, and His testimonies, according to what is written in the Law of Moses, that you may succeed in all that you do and wherever you turn...

1 Kings 2:3 (NASB)

But seek first His kingdom and His righteousness, and all these things will be added to you.

Matthew 6:33 (NASB)

DAY 20

When to Say No to Giving

The other day I received this email from a reader...

"Hi Bob,
When is it ok to say no in your giving? It seems
through my giving I have gained a reputation of
being a bank to some needy people. I myself am in
debt and seem to give more than take care of my
own needs. These same people have come to
expect me to give and some have even demanded
that I give more than I have to give. I admit I am
becoming irritated and have told some of them in
irritation that I am not their personal piggy bank.
However, I feel guilty for turning them away. Is my
limit to giving a sin? I know Jesus implores us to
have compassion on those less fortunate,
especially when we have huge financial needs. I

am understanding His Kingdom economics and ask His forgiveness if my giving is done out of duty and irritation."

While this is a touchy subject, I wanted to share this because I think it's something that many Christians need help with.

I strongly advocate giving and think that it's one of the best things we can do with our lives. But, I believe there's a wrong and a right way to give.

Personally, I have seen a few too many people give under compulsion - which scripture clearly tells us to avoid.

But without your consent I wanted to do nothing, that your good deed might not be by compulsion, as it were, but voluntary.

Philemon 1:14 (NASB)

Each of you must give what you have decided in your heart, not with regret or under compulsion, since God loves a cheerful giver.

2 Corinthians 9.7 (NASB)

Also, I don't get too excited when I see people go in

debt in order to give to someone.

While the intentions are probably good, is it really giving if you don't have it to give?

DAY 21

God's Economy

God's promises are not contingent on the state of the U.S. economy!

I'm not sure if you need to hear this, but I have days when I need a gentle reminder. As Christians, we are children of God and aren't limited by the circumstances around us. We have God's promises that He is going to provide for us, no matter what it looks like.

Our job is to simply believe. As Bono put it in *Walk On*, "(it) has to be believed to be seen."

We all would love to see things manifest and then believe them, but remember what Jesus said to Thomas?

Is it because you have seen me that you have

believed? How blessed are those who have never
seen me and yet have believed!

John 20:29 (NIV)

God's economy is strong

I believe that we should be paying down our
debts in response to the economy's challenges. As
far as our stewardship goes, I think this is a good
practical step for us to take. But even great
stewards still need to trust God to meet their
needs.

I am praying for our nation that the economic
challenges will clear up, but either way, I know I
have to trust God. If I really believe God is my
supply and source, then I should feel just as
confident that He will meet my needs when they
look good as when they look terrible.

The truth is that God's economy is strong and will
never go into a depression or even a recession.
God is not short on cash, and He's a great father
who takes care of his kids.

And these are a few more important things that we
need to remember...

God promised to supply all of our needs

It doesn't matter whether it's a bear market, bull market, recession, depression, or anything else. This promise from Philippians 4:19 is not contingent on what the government is doing, the economy, or even our own ability. It's a promise from the only source in the universe that we can rest assured is going to back up what He promised.

Trusting in God is key

It's so easy to look at our checkbooks, credit card statements, IRAs, or 401ks and get discouraged. But, God isn't discouraged or even surprised at what's going on. He didn't promise that we would never have challenges or that, at times, things would look bad. But He did say He would never leave us or forsake us (see Hebrews 13:5-6) and wants us to feel encouraged by His faithfulness. Our job as Christians is to continue to trust Him regardless of whether things look good or bad.

It is faith that pleases God

In fact, the Bible says that, without faith, it's IMPOSSIBLE to please Him (see Hebrews 11:6).

Whether I like it or not, the biggest faith tests are rarely when circumstances are going very well but are when things look bad or even impossible. The super-encouraging thing about this is that when I just keep on trusting God when things look bad, I'm very pleasing to Him!

DAY 22

The Complacency of Fools

...and the complacency of fools shall destroy them.

Proverbs 1:32 (NASB)

I was doing a little bit of studying on this verse and I looked up the definition of complacent. Webster's definition surprised me. The first definition was "self-satisfied," and the third was "unconcerned."

I had never thought of this verse in this way. I had always just assumed complacent meant lazy. These definitions of the word shine a new light on it for me. When I think of someone who is self-satisfied, I think of someone who has accomplished something. A truly lazy person probably wouldn't have much to feel self-satisfied about, but what I'm getting from this verse is that even if we had accomplishments in the past, we cannot rest on our laurels.

All roads lead to Rome

It reminds me of how Rome fell. It wasn't because they were lazy. I'm sure a lot of energy was spent becoming the powerhouse of the world that it was. But, it fell (though some historians argue) because they became self-satisfied or complacent.

What does this mean for us?

I'm always amazed at how quickly we can adapt to situations. You know the old story that a frog will jump out of a pot of boiling water, but will keep swimming if you increase the heat slowly? I'm keeping my eyes open for the areas in my life where complacency may set in. I often find that if I'm getting a bit too comfortable in an area, I might need to step it up a bit.

DAY 23

Receiving God's Blessings

I'm currently reading through the New Testament with the Message Bible. It's a popular modern translation that tries to bring the essence of what the Bible says into today's language. I enjoy reading it to see certain scriptures in a different light. As I was reading yesterday, one popped out to me:

What I'm trying to do here is get you to relax, not be so preoccupied with getting so you can respond to God's giving.

Luke 12:29 (MSG)

It seems to me that when I'm focused on getting, I often miss what God is trying to give me.

I can remember times I was so focused on what I wanted and how I could get it, that I was blind to the fact that God was answering my prayer in a better, but different, way than I expected. In fact, I would say that most of my great breakthroughs God delivered in a way I didn't expect at all. He seems to get a kick out of doing that.

Getting often involves taking something with force, rather than receiving what God gives us. God loves to give us gifts and wants to bless us. The challenge is to wait to receive from Him rather than taking things with our own energy and our own force.

I wrote an article about this a while ago. In it, I talked about how using credit cards could be robbing us of a blessing. If we pray and ask God to provide something for us, we could be stealing an opportunity for God to bless us in a special and unique way if we just run out and charge it just because we don't want to wait.

The keys, of course, are trusting God and having the patience to wait for it. I know I have jumped the gun and missed it more times than I can count, but it's a personal goal of mine to become more of a receiver of God's blessings and less of an impatient taker.

DAY 24

5 Lessons from the Garden about Bearing Fruit

The fruit of the Spirit

Who doesn't want to be more loving, joyful, at peace, patient, kind, full of goodness, faithful, gentle, and self-controlled? Each of those qualities are the fruit the Bible says we should bear (John 15:16). I know I would love to see each one of them more in my own life – wouldn't you? So, what do we need to do to bear more fruit?

1. Fruit needs water in order to reach its fullest potential

You can probably ask your five-year-old how to take care of a plant, and he will tell you that it needs water to survive. And if you have ever kept a garden, you surely realize that if you only water it once a week during the summer months your harvest will yield much less. On the other hand, if your plants receive frequent and consistent watering, the plants are stronger, and the fruit is better.

He is like a tree planted by streams of water, which yields its fruit in season and whose leaf does not wither. Whatever he does prospers.

Psalm 1:3 (NIV)

2. Good soil is very important

The soil contains a lot of the nutrients that help plants to grow. There are tremendous differences between good soil and bad soil. We need to be spiritually receptive to allow the seeds of God's word to grow and develop the way they should.

The one who received the seed that fell on good soil is the man who hears the word and understands it. He produces a crop, yielding a hundred, sixty or thirty times what was sown.

Matthew 13:23 (NIV)

3. Death brings life

I tell you the truth, unless a kernel of wheat falls to the ground and dies, it remains only a single seed. But if it dies, it produces many seeds.

John 12:24 (NIV)

We must let ourselves and our own desires die and submit to God's plan. In doing so, as the verse states, we will bear much fruit.

4. Pruning produces more fruit

I am by no means an expert gardener, but I have found this one true. It doesn't make sense while you're doing it, but the results prove its effectiveness. God is an expert gardener, and He knows which areas of our lives He can prune to make us more effective. It does hurt, but the end result is beautiful.

He cuts off every branch in me that bears no fruit, while every branch that does bear fruit he prunes so that it will be even more fruitful.

5. A branch can't bear fruit separated from the plant

That's a no-brainer, right? Well, I don't know about you, but I've caught myself trying to do that in my own life. I will find myself trying to accomplish things with my own strength rather than "abiding in Him." All the fruit that we bear in our lives will result from us having a connection to our source: God. Just like a severed branch can bear no fruit, neither can we bear any fruit if we don't abide in Him.

I am the vine; you are the branches. If a man remains in me and I in him, he will bear much fruit; apart from me you can do nothing.

John 15:5 (NIV)

DAY 25

Don't Act Like the Foolish Virgins

Just as with all the parables Jesus used to teach valuable lessons, there's some wisdom to be gained from the parable of the 10 virgins.

As with most things in life, some were wise, some were foolish, and both reaped what they sowed. I have posted the whole parable below as a refresher...

At that time the kingdom of heaven will be like ten virgins who took their lamps and went out to meet the bridegroom. Five of them were foolish and five were wise.
The foolish ones took their lamps but did not take any oil with them. The wise, however, took oil in

jars along with their lamps. The bridegroom was a long time in coming, and they all became drowsy and fell asleep.

At midnight the cry rang out: "Here's the bridegroom! Come out to meet him!"

Then all the virgins woke up and trimmed their lamps. The foolish ones said to the wise, "Give us some of your oil; our lamps are going out."

"No," they replied, " There may not be enough for both us and you. Instead, go to those who sell oil and buy some for yourselves."

But while they were on their way to buy the oil, the bridegroom arrived. The virgins who were ready went in with him to the wedding banquet. And the door was shut. Later the others also came. "Sir! Sir!" they said. "Open the door for us!' But he replied, "I tell you the truth, I don't know you." Therefore keep watch, because you do not know the day or the hour.

Matthew 25:1-13 (NIV)

Five wise virgins

There are a lot of lessons to be learned from this parable, but to me, the biggest lesson I learned is to get prepared! I think this can apply to all areas of life, including our finances.

So what should you prepare for?

I have noticed that most people drastically under-prepare for situations or they over-prepare. The key is to stay balanced.

Preparation is not to be something that's guided by fear, but by wisdom. The Bible says that God hasn't given us a spirit of fear. (See 2 Timothy 1:7.) Therefore, we shouldn't make our decisions based on fear.

So, if you're preparing for situations, first make sure that you're trusting God and not doing it because you're afraid.

These are just a few things the parable of the virgins has helped inspire me to prepare for.

An emergency fund

This is one of the first things that Dave Ramsey recommends to do in *The Total Money Makeover*, and I completely agree. In order to have a fighting chance of getting out of debt, you should have an emergency fund started. The purpose, of course, is to allow you to handle car problems, a blown water heater, or any other urgent and unexpected expense.

Retirement savings

We shouldn't be saving everything for retirement, but we probably all should save something. The goal isn't to hoard wealth for the last 30 years of our lives, but to share it!

Whether you plan on staying in your current job until you die, preparation allows you to have options. When I'm 70, I want to get paid for doing something I love, rather than having to go to work to pay the bills.

A disaster

After Hurricane Katrina hit the Gulf Coast a few years ago, I decided to take some steps to prepare for a natural disaster. After the hurricane, some of our neighbors in the South had a few weeks of living in the "Wild West."

They didn't have water, power, an easy way to get food, or ATMs they could run to.
As we near the end times, we're going to see more of these types of occurrences, and it would be wise of us to prepare.

Obviously preparing a disaster kit is a good way to prepare. We also have stashed some cash in case ATM networks stop functioning.

The foolish virgins

The five foolish virgins missed out on a great opportunity. The reason they missed out was because they weren't prepared! I think we heed to this warning and take action by preparing for the things we know we should.

Remember how Joseph prepared for the seven years of famine (see Genesis 41)?

What would have happened if he decided not to prepare, saying to himself, "I don't need to prepare. God will take care of me."? I don't know the answer, but it's interesting to think about.

DAY 26

The Hardest Financial Habit to Break

Breaking the habit of discontentment

I was recently asked what the most difficult habit to break was as I started getting my finances in order. I think, for me, it was breaking the habit of discontentment. I used to see something I wanted, and I would want it so much I wouldn't be happy until I got it.

It has taken a while to break this bad habit and replace it with a good one, but I really believe it's one of the most valuable moves I made as far as my finances go. Even though it's still something I fight like everyone else, the progress made so far has proved tremendously valuable.

Discontentment is rampant in the U.S. culture and increasing in other parts of the world. The Bible says that the eyes of a man are never satisfied (Proverbs 27:20), so getting more stuff is not the cure, but actually the source of the problem.

As creatures of habit, we're used to getting whatever we want, so it will just make it that much harder to tell ourselves NO. But, if we're not programmed to get a new car every other year, a new wardrobe each season, or a bigger house to impress our friends, then it's much easier to stay content with what we have.

My lack of contentment was also what drove me to spend more than I earned. I was earning more than enough to live a nice life, but I wasn't content with what I had. I wanted more.

It wasn't until I started slapping myself around a bit and telling myself NO, that I began to actually be thankful for what I had. I was finally enjoying the things I had, rather than just chasing after the newest toy on the market.

DAY 27

Why You Should Get out of Debt

I just don't get why anyone would choose to get in debt. Mathematically, I understand the advantages of leveraging debt, but math doesn't explain every situation. As emotional creatures, we don't function as walking calculators making every decision based solely on the numbers.

While math plays a role in our financial lives, there are far more powerful truths, like discipline, for example. The thing is that most of us know mathematically what we should do with our finances, yet because of a lack of discipline we don't do it. So, what then needs fixing – the math or the discipline?

Another truth that really clarified for me why I needed to get out of debt is that the Bible says, "the borrower is slave to the lender."

Anyone who has been in deep debt can attest to the truth of this. Essentially, when you dig yourself into debt, you give up control of your life. With each new debt, you give more control to your lender and slowly become more of a slave.

You don't have to be in debt

I always thought that debt was just a way of life. I accepted the fact that I would always have a car payment. Everyone has credit cards, so I just assumed if everyone was doing it, it was okay. Then something changed. I decided that rather than always having a car payment, I wanted to never take out a loan on a car again. Sure, in the short term I might not drive the car of my dreams, but what I found was the little sacrifice has continued and will continue to yield tremendous fruit.

Think about it – most of the companies advertising have some form of credit or financing they offer. So, everything we hear from them is going to try to convince us that being in debt is normal, fun, and what the "cool kids are doing."

It may be normal, but there's something so much better available to us.

Freedom

One of my greatest motivators for becoming debt-free has been the freedom. I just can't wait until I have every debt paid off and actually OWN my home. Paying bills will be so fun!

I just sit and smile when I think about the freedom of not living paycheck to paycheck. I used to live in fear knowing that if I were out of work for more than a week, I would be in big trouble financially. Personally, I don't believe that God set us free in so many other areas, so that we could stay slaves in the area of debt.

Others are affected

On my journey to get out of debt, I discovered that the reason for it is a lot larger than my freedom. While that has been a great motivator for me, I now get excited about the increased opportunity to give. Almost everyone has experienced the joy of giving. The challenge is that we often want to give but have all these other necessary expenses that have to be taken out first. If you're like most, it seems as if there's never quite as much to give as you would like.

This is exactly why we need to get out from under our debt. How can we expect to be big givers if we owe money to everyone else and don't have anything ourselves?

Personally, I'm not satisfied with how much I currently give. I have a feeling that I'm not alone in this. I believe that a lot of churches are limited in their ability to give because of debt. I believe that God wants something more from us. I believe that He wants us to become good stewards of our finances so that we can better honor Him and others with our checkbooks.

DAY 28

Budgeting for Giving

If giving is better than receiving, why doesn't it feel like it?

I remember when I was strapped for cash and needed to buy someone a birthday gift - it didn't FEEL like much of a blessing as the giver.

I hated the feeling of being torn with what to do with my money. I wanted to be a generous giver, but when the $20 in my wallet was pulled in four different directions, it was difficult to be as generous as I wanted.

I'm not sure where I got the idea from, but we had a very basic budget at the time and decided to create a budget account specifically for gifts and giving. This account was to be the source of all our birthday and Christmas presents and any other giving we did.

I thought it was a good idea until we started doing it. Then I realized that it was an absolutely GREAT idea and wish we had started it earlier. It instantly added so much more fun to the giving process, because the money was just sitting there waiting for us to spend it on others. It wasn't pulled in numerous directions as it was previously. Its purpose was clearly defined.

Christians are called to give

We have the opportunity to give into God's kingdom. We have the privilege of giving to help people. It really is a privilege and an opportunity. God doesn't need us. He has an endless supply of finances. He can get the money where the need is. But He allows us the chance for Him to use us in the process, knowing that WE will benefit from His use.

As we get a better understanding of this truth, it helps us break free from our own selfishness. God really wants to bless us!! He set a system up that's kind of counterintuitive: We give away, and as a result we get more. As we give, we receive in a greater measure. The Bible makes it clear that there's always seedtime and harvest. To the measure that we sow, we will reap.

Biblical giving

After we started to get an understanding about Biblical giving, we faced the same challenges everyone else does. You want to give, but it's hard to find money to give, because it's already spent on other important things.

It was for this reason that we had to start budgeting for our giving. The Bible says that we are to "discipline ourselves for the purpose of godliness" and that "we should not make any provision for the flesh."

It is crucial that we set up NATURAL processes and habits in order to fulfill the SPIRITUAL things we're called to do.

In this case taking money right off the top of our income to budget for giving were the natural steps that helped fulfill what God wanted us to do. It wasn't enough that we wanted to give or even that we asked God to help us give. We had to take natural steps (that were His will) to fulfill what He wanted us to do.

<u>Bottom Line:</u> Budgeting for giving was just a simple step that helped us fulfill what we were called to do.

A few things that budgeting for gifts did for us:

- Assuming we were adding enough to the account, we rarely (if ever) would need to try to find money to purchase gifts.
- It encouraged more generosity because money was sitting in the account just waiting to be spent.
- We agreed it would ONLY be used for giving purposes, therefore we might as well spend it because that was what it was there for.

It's a wonderful feeling to have money available for the sole purpose of blessing others. It makes it really EASY and FUN to give.

It's great to have cash always available to pay for birthday gifts, but it's even more exciting as you increase your budgeted amount. When it gets to the point that there's so much money in the account that you have to start looking for people to bless, it really begins to become fun!

Before we started budgeting for gifts, I never had a

thorough understanding of what Jesus meant that it was more blessed to give than to receive. The main reason was that giving created a negative side effect on my finances.

Since I purchased groceries and gifts from money in the same pot, I was always torn between my desire to give and my desire to eat.

Now, instead of thinking about how a gift would prevent me from getting more groceries, I now am free to focus on blessing the other person rather than my grocery list.

If you haven't tried it, you should!

DAY 29

Are You a Good Steward?

Back in Day 10 we talked a bit about stewardship, but it is such an important topic that I wanted to bring it up again.

The Bible says that someone who is faithful with a little thing will be faithful with much (Luke 16:9-11). So, if we are honest and do the right thing when no one is looking, we're trustworthy when people are looking.

The basic message that I have gotten from the Bible about being a good steward is that God has entrusted me with things on earth, and it is my responsibility to do something good with them.

Being a good steward

Realize that God owns it all. It's easy to forget that God created the world we live in and us, as well. He created the air we breathe, the sun that warms the earth, and plants and animals for food. He's the one who gave us our brains to think; he placed different gifts and skills in each one of us and gave us each unique personalities.

It is only because of His great mercy that he doesn't just prove to me how dependent I am on Him when I start to think I really accomplished something on my own. As we understand that "the earth is the Lord's and everything in it," (Psalms 24:1) we can see that we're merely temporary possessors (or stewards) of things He owns.

We are born with nothing, and we take nothing with us when we leave. It all just gets passed on to someone else. The amazing thing is that we have the opportunity to "store up for ourselves treasures in heaven" by giving some of those items that we temporarily possess down here.

Stewards can serve only one master

No one can serve two masters. Either he will hate

*the one and love the other, or he will be devoted to
the one and despise the other. You cannot serve
both God and money.*

Matthew 6:24 (NIV)

I've found from my own life that my decisions
about money reflect who I'm serving. At the most
stingy and greedy moments of my life, it was
painfully evident who my master was. I tried to
convince myself that I was serving God, but in
truth, my decisions were made on their financial
impact rather than on my faith in God. It's one of
those areas that we will all have room to grow in.

I remember patting myself on the back after an act
of generosity that I was proud of, only to be shown,
moments later, two other areas of my life that I was
greedy in. It's humbling, but it's also encouraging
to know that we will never "arrive," and that God
doesn't expect that of us.

He knows our weaknesses and our strengths. He
knows what we're capable of and while I earnestly
want to please Him, I'm so thankful for His
forgiveness when I mess up.

Use resources wisely

As stewards we have a responsibility to use what we've received wisely. Just as in the parable of the talents, it is up to us how we use what we have. We can choose to bury it like the "lazy" steward, or we can make more from what we have like the "good" stewards.

As far as managing our finances goes, there's a tricky balance between not being wasteful like Jesus talks about in John 6:12 and not living with a poverty mindset. It's easy to lean toward one of the extremes, and it's challenging to walk in balance. That balance is what we should be seeking in the practical areas of being stewards of our finances.

The great thing is that as we prove ourselves faithful in small things, we will be given more and bigger things to be stewards over.

His master replied, "Well done, good and faithful servant! You have been faithful with a few things; I will put you in charge of many things. Come and share your master's happiness!"

Matthew 25:21-22 (NIV)

DAY 30

Are You Free from the Love of Money?

I was recently listening to a preacher who was saying something that really grabbed my attention. He made a great point based on the verse below:

But those who want to get rich fall into temptation and a snare and many foolish and harmful desires which plunge men into ruin and destruction. For the love of money is a root of all sorts of evil, and some by longing for it have wandered away from the faith and pierced themselves with many griefs. But flee from these things, you man of God, and pursue righteousness, godliness, faith, love, perseverance and gentleness.

1 Timothy 6:9-11 (NASB)

This is written to those who don't have money as much as those who do.

The Bible says that man looks at the outward appearance, but God looks at the heart. God knows our thoughts and motivations behind every action we take. People, on the other hand, do not, but they like to think they do. It's easy to look at someone with a lot of money and judge them quoting the above verse. But we will NEVER know the heart.

But, some people who don't have much money, who would probably never be judged for being in love with money, could be completely guilty in God's eyes of lusting after wealth.

The truth is, I have known people who didn't have much money who would have done anything to get money. They would lie, steal, cheat, and hurt anyone who got in the way just to get money. This is a condition of the heart. We all know that there are many rich people who behave exactly the same way. If they did it when they were poor, they will do it when they're rich.

I have also known millionaires who spent most of their time trying to bless others. They were moral role-models who did not make their decisions based on how it would affect them financially, but by what would be pleasing to God. Not being God, I can't know for sure the condition of their heart, but from seeing their behavior I can safely assume they were not those being described in the verse above.

Be content

The preacher I heard was telling a story about how he had not worked in more than a year, had no income, and in the middle of that situation, God started to show him that he had a materialism issue to deal with. The guy argued with God saying, "I don't have any money, how can I be materialistic?" He quickly realized:

1. God was right, and he did have an issue.
2. His materialism was tied to his discontentment.

The apostle Paul talked about how he learned how to "abase and abound," how he could live in high times and low times. He had figured out how to be content with whatever he had. He understood that God was his supply and that God would meet his needs. He understood that if he sought the Kingdom of God first that the "things" would follow.

Once we break free from the mindset that "life will be so much better when..." we will truly be free. God wants us to be content NOW. He doesn't want us to wait until our circumstances change for the better to be content...

Make sure that your character is free from the love of money, being content with what you have; for He Himself has said, "I WILL NEVER DESERT YOU, NOR WILL I EVER FORSAKE YOU

Hebrews 13:5 (NASB)

DAY 31

The Most Important Thing to Remember about Money

As I sat searching the Word this morning for comfort, I was reminded of this crucial piece of wisdom that had drifted from my memory. Over the years, I have probably written about it in articles or emails a dozen times. But still, I constantly need to remind myself because it's so easy to forget.

What's more is when I, or anyone really, forget about it, it causes a lot of undue stress that can be greatly minimized when we truly understand this one simple thing.

So what is this thing about money we should never forget?

It's all God's money, and He is allowing us use it!

If you read the Parable of the Talents, you get a great illustration of how we are supposed to view money: it's all God's money, and we just get to be managers of it in this life. It doesn't matter whether we have a little or a lot. We came into the world with nothing, and we aren't taking any of it with us. We have the opportunity for God to use us with our finances as long as we get out of the way!

I recently found myself getting all caught up in "my money," and it caused me a lot of unnecessary stress. As soon as I was reminded of this simple fact, it instantaneously changed how I viewed a tricky financial issue.

When it isn't "our" money, but God's, the weight of the responsibility shifts from us to Him. And this is exactly where it should be. God designed us to depend on Him. We are co-laborers and have a part to play in the process – but let's be real, God's words frame the whole universe. If He forgot about us for half a second, we would be goners.

Let's let this be a reminder for us all. Whether

things are tough financially right now or going well, it doesn't matter - our proper role is to be a dependent steward of whatever He has entrusted to us!

Thanks For Reading!

I just want to thank you for devoting the time to stick with this book.

I hope you found it helpful, and either way I'd love to hear your feedback. So, don't be a stranger and stop by SeedTime.com to got signed up for one of our free email courses.

I appreciate you more than you know, and I wish you all the best in your journey!

Bob

34282551R00074

Printed in Great Britain
by Amazon